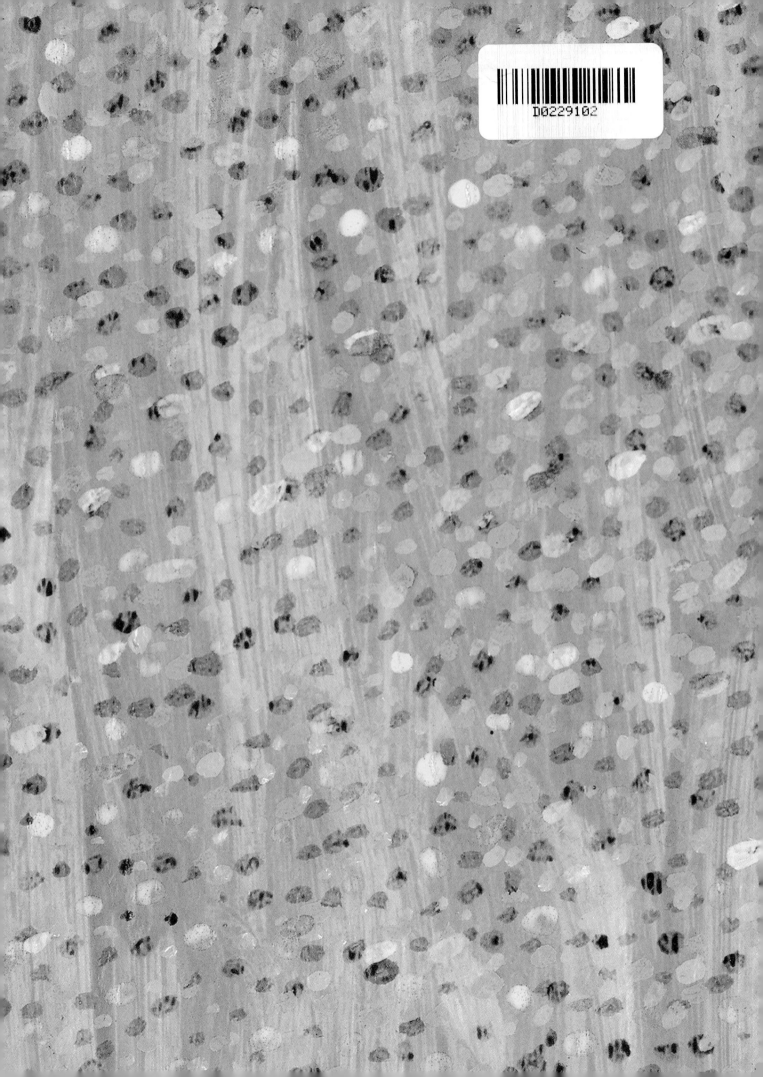

the very hungry caterpillar and friends
my very first annual

This book belongs to

....

PUFFIN

PUFFIN BOOKS
Published by the Penguin Group: London, New York, Australia,
Canada, India, Ireland, New Zealand and South Africa
Penguin Books Ltd, Registered Offices: 80 Strand, London WC2R 0RL, England

puffinbooks.com

This collection published in Great Britain in Puffin Books 2010
1 3 5 7 9 10 8 6 4 2

Made and printed in China
ISBN: 978-0-141-33289-5

To find out more about Eric Carle books, visit www.eric-carle.com
To find out about The Eric Carle Museum of Picture Book Art,
visit www.picturebookart.org

contents

Are you hungry? The Very Hungry Caterpillar certainly is! As he eats his way through the week, **count** all the fruits and treats using the **giant** stickers to finish the pictures.

count

with
The Very Hungry Caterpillar

In the light of the moon

a little egg lay on a leaf.

One Sunday morning the warm sun came up and – pop! – out of the egg came a tiny and very hungry caterpillar.

He started to look for some food.

On Monday he ate through one apple.
But he was still hungry.

On Tuesday he ate through two pears, but he was still hungry.

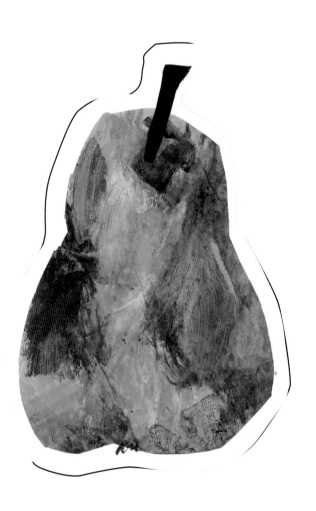
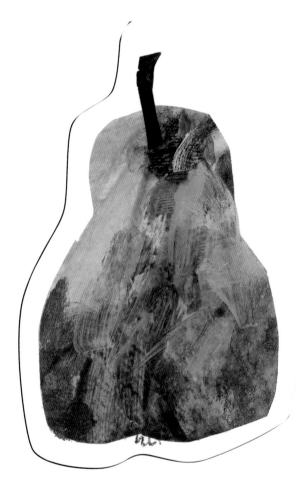

On Wednesday he ate through
three plums, but he was still hungry.

On Thursday he ate through four strawberries, but he was still hungry.

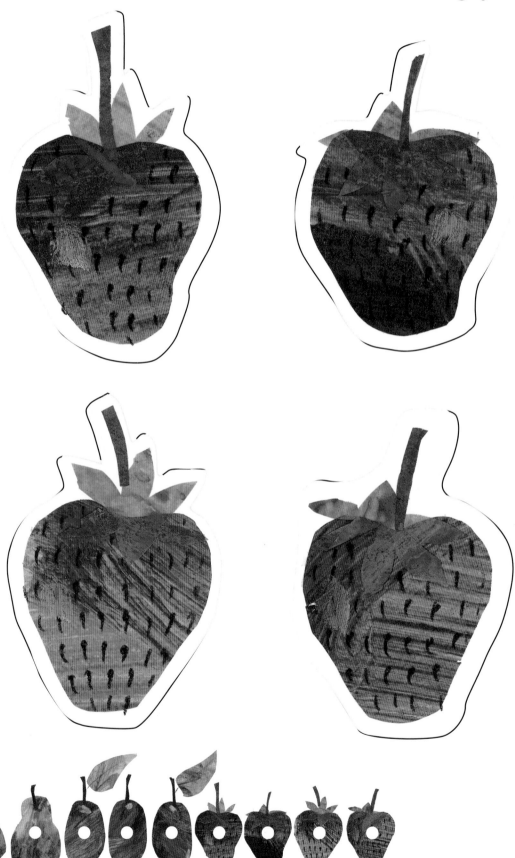

On Friday he ate through five
oranges, but he was still hungry.

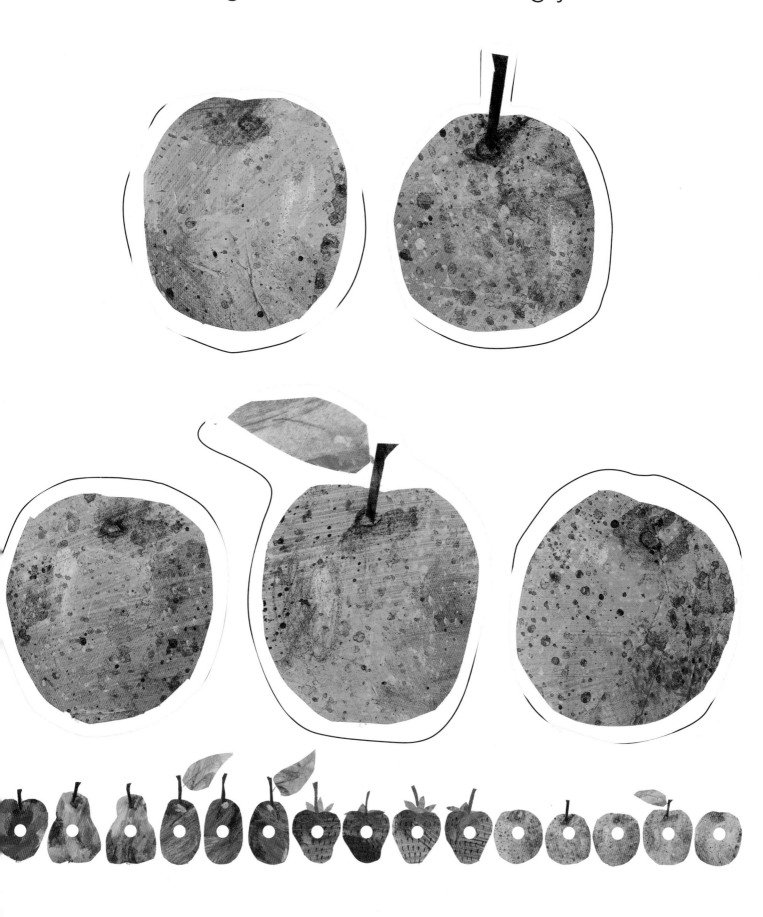

On Saturday he ate through one piece
of chocolate cake, one ice-cream cone,
one pickle, one slice of Swiss cheese,

one slice of salami, one lollipop, one piece of cherry pie, one sausage, one cupcake, and one slice of watermelon.

That night he had a stomachache!

The next day was Sunday again. The caterpillar ate through one nice green leaf, and after that he felt much better.

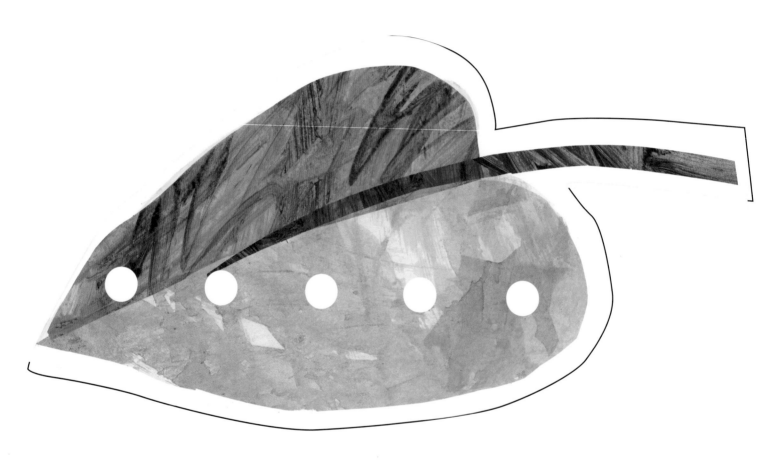

Now he wasn't hungry any more – and he wasn't a little caterpillar any more. He was a big, fat caterpillar.

He built a small house, called a
cocoon, around himself. He stayed
inside for more than two weeks.

Then he nibbled a hole in the cocoon,
pushed his way out and . . .

he was a beautiful butterfly!

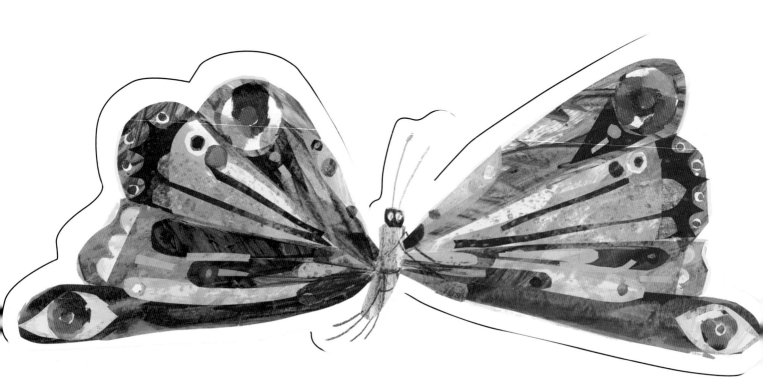

The Very Lonely Firefly is very lonely.
Fly with him through the night to find his
friends, and use the **glittery** stickers
along the way.

shine

with
The Very Lonely Firefly

As the sun set
a little firefly was born.
It stretched its wings
and flew off
into the darkening sky.

It was a lonely firefly
and it flashed its light,
searching for other fireflies.

The firefly saw a light
and flew towards it.

But it was not another firefly.
It was a light bulb
lighting up the night.

The firefly saw a light
and flew towards it.

But it was not another firefly.
It was a candle
flickering in the night.

The firefly saw a light
and flew towards it.

But it was not another firefly.
It was a lantern
glowing in the night.

The firefly saw a light
and flew towards it.

But it was not another firefly.
It was a flashlight
shining in the night.

The firefly saw several lights
and flew towards them.
But they were not other fireflies.

an owl, their eyes reflecting the lights.

The firefly saw many lights
and flew towards them.

But they were not other fireflies.

They were fireworks
sparkling and glittering
and shimmering in the night.

When all was quiet, the firefly flew
through the night flashing its light,
looking and searching again.

Then the very lonely firefly saw what it had been looking for . . .

A group of fireflies, flashing *their* lights.

Now the firefly wasn't lonely any more.

Here are the giant and glittery stickers
for count with The Very Hungry Caterpillar
and shine with The Very Lonely Firefly.

Use these stickers for **Count with The Very Hungry Caterpillar**

Use these stickers for **Count with The Very Hungry Caterpillar**

Use these stickers for **Count with The Very Hungry Caterpillar**

colouring

with

1, 2, 3 to the Zoo

The animals are on their way to the Zoo.
Colour and count and come along too!

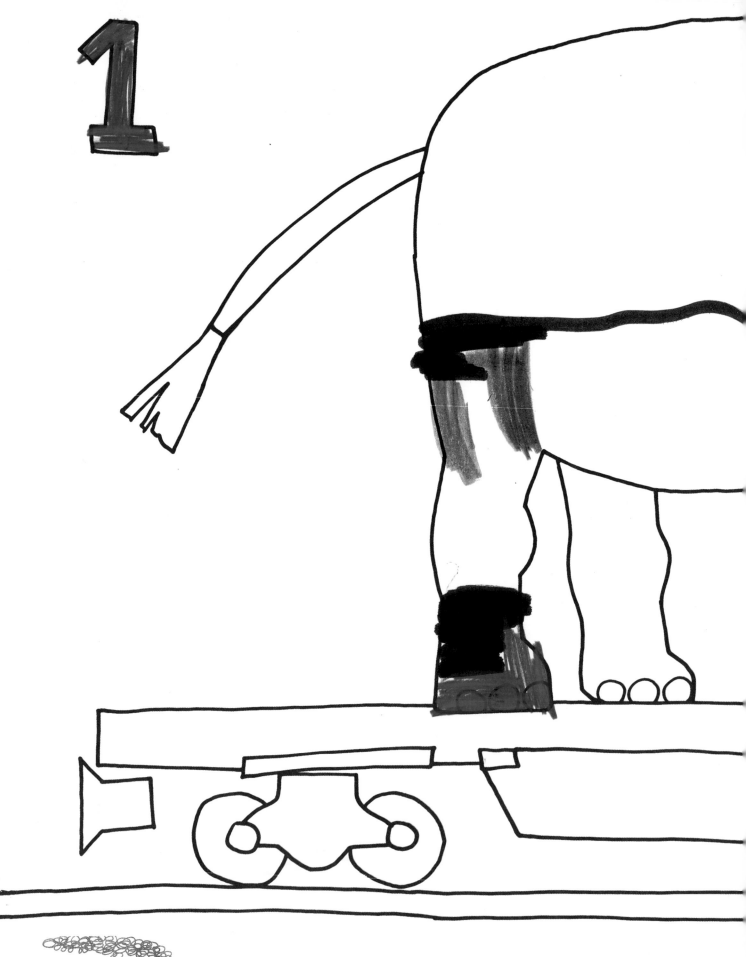

2

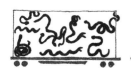

How many animals are in each railway carriage?

   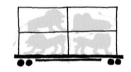 

1   2   3   4   5

___   ___   ___   ___   ___

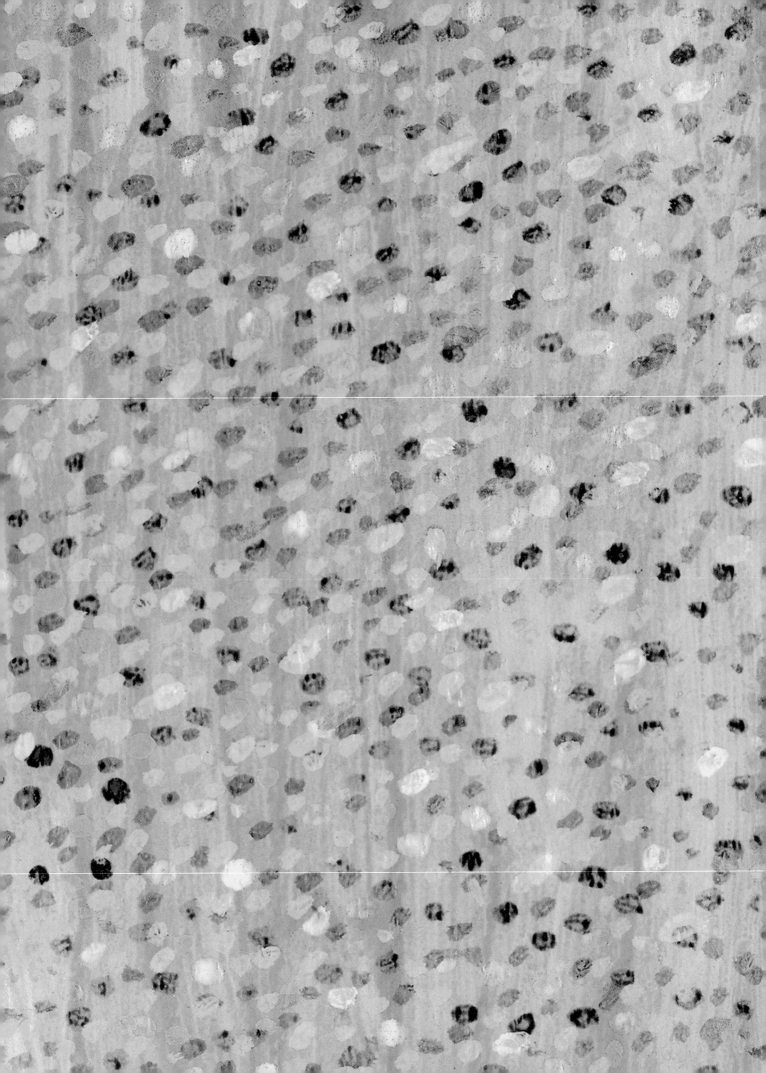